inkblots

For Elementary Creative Writing

4-6

by
Pat Watson and Janet Watson

ecs

Editor: Cherisse Mastry
Page Layout & Graphics: Cherisse Mastry & Kirstin Simpson
Cover/Book Design: Educational Media Services

These popular series of books are available from ECS Learning Systems, Inc.

The Math Whiz Kids™	Gr. 3-5	4 Titles
The Little Red Writing Book	Ages 6-12	3 Titles
The Bright Blue Thinking Book	Ages 6-12	3 Titles
Structures for Reading, Writing, Thinking	Gr. 4-9	4 Titles
Writing Warm-Ups™	Gr. K-6	2 Titles
Foundations for Writing	Gr. 2-8	2 Titles
Springboards for Reading	Gr. 3-6	1 Title
Booklinks to American and World History	Gr. 4-8	12 Titles
Novel Extenders	Gr. 1-6	7 Titles
Building Language Power	Gr. 4-9	3 Titles
Quick Thinking™	Gr. K-12	2 Titles
Thematic Units	Gr. K-8	23 Titles
Activity Books	Gr. K-12	11 Titles
EnviroLearn™	Gr. K-5	5 Titles
Home Study Collection™ (Basic Skills & More)	Gr. 1-6	18 Titles
Test Preparation Guides	Gr. 2-12	41 Titles
Passageways	Gr. 5-9	1 Title
Booklinks	Gr. 3-8	1 Title
Tactics to Tackle Thinking	Gr. 6-12	1 Title

To order, contact your local school supply store, or write for a complete catalog:

ECS Learning Systems, Inc.
P.O. Box 791437
San Antonio, Texas 78279-1437

ISBN 1-57022-180-4

© **1998 by ECS Learning Systems, Inc., San Antonio, Texas.** All rights reserved. No part of this publication may be reproduced, stored in a retrieval system, or transmitted in any way or by any means (electronic, mechanical, photocopying, recording, or otherwise) without prior written permission from ECS Learning Systems, Inc., with the exceptions found below.

Photocopying of student worksheets by a teacher who purchased this publication for his/her own class is permissible. Reproduction of any part of this publication for an entire school or for a school system or for commercial sale is strictly prohibited. **Copyright infringement is a violation of Federal Law.**

Printed in the United States of America.

Acknowledgments

Thanks to Kimberly Keller, art teacher, Georgetown ISD (Georgetown, TX) for contributing to the section, Writing Stages (p. 14).

Thanks to Pat Benson, retired science teacher, Muleshoe ISD (Muleshoe, TX) and Temple ISD (Temple, TX) for the suggested grading criteria used for monitoring peer response groups (p. 32). She now resides in College Station, Texas.

Thanks to our students, who inspired us to develop creative ideas to challenge their thinking and writing skills.

Table of Contents

Preface

Getting Started   9
    Word Lists   10
    Activities   12
    Writing Stages   14

Journaling and Letter Writing   19
    Overview   20
    Journal Ideas   22
    Letter Writing   26

Developing a Writing Program   29
    Directives   30
    Peer Response Groups   31
    Guidelines   32

Writing Assignments   35
    Types of Writing   36
    The Writing Process   39
    Preparatory Writing   41
    Descriptive Writing   42
    Narrative Writing   46
    Expository Writing   48
    Persuasive Writing   52

A Closer Look at Stories   55
    Foreword   56
    Story Writing   58
    Writing Books   62
    Autobiographical Writing   66
    Characterizations   68

A Closer Look at Poetry   71
    Poetry Writing   72
    Poetry Notebook   73

Reading and Writing Connection   77
    Assignments   78
       Books to Read Aloud   84
       Additional Assignments   86
       Book Report and Story Summary Ideas   87

Short Assignments   89
    Word Studies   90
       Additional Short Assignments   93
    Collaborative Writing   95

Creative Research   99
    The Research Process   100
    Research Evaluation   104

Student Handouts   107

Student Work   117

About the Authors   127

Preface

Most children have an innate love of words they hear and speak. The goal of elementary creative writing is to capitalize on this love of words and to guide students as they learn to express themselves creatively. The exercises and assignments in *Inkblots for Elementary Creative Writing* are designed to help students express their perceptions as they hear, feel, touch, see, think, and wonder.

This syllabus for grades 4-6 is divided into 11 sections: Getting Started, Journaling and Letter Writing, Developing a Writing Program, Writing Assignments, A Closer Look at Stories, A Closer Look at Poetry, Reading and Writing Connection, Short Assignments, Creative Research, Student Handouts, and Student Work. The Getting Started section includes guidelines to help the teacher understand the writing stages from "scribbling" to accomplished writing. The syllabus features assignments for grades 4-6; however, many of the ideas can be adapted for older or younger students.

Each section is designed to guide teachers to help students think and write creatively. Unit plans in the Writing Assignments section state an objective, focus activity, process for teaching, and assignment. In addition, several lessons include activities and assignment extensions. The Reading and Writing Connection section lists a wide variety of children's books, each with a brief synopsis and accompanying writing assignment.

Assignments include standard writing forms such as paragraphs, stories, and poems. Variations include advertisements, booklets, commercials, editorials, manuals, handbooks, joke books, letters, pamphlets, plays, brochures, picture dictionaries, and newspaper articles.

Teacher participation is a vital part of any creative writing program. Learn to write with your students and enjoy what they have written. As teachers enthusiastically share their own ideas, students come to recognize learning as a never-ending process and writing as a delight.

The material in this book has evolved from many years of teaching creative writing. We hope the ideas in this syllabus inspire you, the teacher, to have fun and to enjoy the "art" of teaching students creative writing.

Getting Started

Word Lists

The activities in this section and the following three sections can be used as springboards for creative writing assignments. Suggested assignments are included when applicable.

Creating word lists should be a class project. Add to the lists as students discover other words. These lists will be useful for various writing assignments. The words can be placed on poster board for use throughout the year or in a card file for easy reference; in addition, students can make their own lists and keep them in a notebook. The length of the list will depend on the students' grade level.

Spelling words: List the correct spelling for commonly used words.

Sound words: List sound words that are nouns (carillons, screams) and adjectives (pealing, piercing).

Career words: List general words (coworkers, promotion, meeting) and specialized words (commuting, policy, troubleshooting) to describe different careers.

Words to describe people: Compile words used to describe people. Include vivid words (vivacious, grotesque, devious, sinister, obese, emaciated, mischievous, compassionate).

Personality words: List words describing personality traits. Include nouns (leader, follower, loner, peacemaker) and adjectives (curious, generous, stubborn, temperamental).

Emotion words: List emotions (jealousy, revenge, sympathy, disappointment, hatred, fear, loneliness, anxiety, happiness, joy, exhilaration).

Category words: Create a list of words that describe a category: musical instruments, modes of transportation, occupations, foods, toys, tools, feelings, buildings, furniture, sports, age groups (children, teenagers, adults), topics (family, school).

Lazy words: List words that are overused and make writing dull. For example, include nouns (girl, boy), adjectives (good, bad, big, little, pretty, best), adverbs (very, really, too), and verbs (got, love, ran).

Dynamic words: List unusual words, similes, metaphors, vivid descriptive words, and strong action verbs.

Connecting words: List words that connect compound or compound/complex sentences (because, if, however, therefore, so, when, while, but, and, although, since), or words that introduce an idea (first, last, second) and connect paragraphs.

Variation: Homonym, synonym, and antonym lists can be created as an alternative activity or assignment.

Activities

Idea Boxes

To create idea boxes, mount material on index cards; create card files for the following short assignments.

Headlines can be a class project for younger students or an individual project for older students. Have students choose an unusual headline and create a story that fits the headline. Read some of the students' stories aloud, then read the original article and compare. File original stories.

Advertisements: Select an advertisement with colorful pictures. Cut away the message, and have students create an original advertisement, either as a class project or individually.

Picture Files

1. Collect pictures from magazines, mount them on heavy paper, and laminate them.

2. Write questions on the back of each picture to stimulate creative thinking.

3. Include photos of people showing a variety of emotions (babies' expressions lead to wonderful, creative ideas), animals in natural and unusual habitats, insects, landscapes, foods, occupations, household items, unusual objects, weather (storm clouds, lightning).

Picture Files can encompass a wide variety of ideas. Form questions around why, what, how, where, sequence, predicted outcomes, realism/fantasy, etc.

Variation: Display a picture of a spaceship, or have students bring one to class as the previous day's homework assignment. Create a specific assignment for Picture Files. Example: It is the year 3000. You are aboard this spaceship bound for Mars with three other people. Write a narrative of your journey. Additional writing assignments can include descriptive, expository, narrative, or persuasive writing.

Writing Stages

Students come into our classrooms with a variety of backgrounds and skills. Through understanding the stages of writing development, teachers can identify specific needs of individual students and monitor writing improvement on an individual basis.

Stage One: Beginning Writing

- Scribbles randomly*
- Acts as if (s)he can read what has been written
- Scribbles with some sense of direction
- Forms letters
- Writes own name (often in all capital letters)
- Copies what someone has written
- Dictates words or short phrases (for objects, pictures, experiences)

Stage Two: Writing Words

- Writes family names (Mom, Dad)
- Shows some understanding of word length
- Understands spaces between words
- Is unconcerned with spelling and/or punctuation

Stage Three: New Words/Short Phrases

- Writes new words
- Completes pattern sentences with word or phrase: "I am…."; "That is a…."; "I like…."
- Writes short caption (two or three words) for picture
- Writes simple phrases

---

* Any scribbling is a step forward in the child's realization that marks on paper can be read; a communication value; a prewriting sign.

Stage Four: Simple Sentences

- Composes sentences by following the pattern of a model sentence
- Writes simple, unrelated sentences

Stage Five: Combines Sentences into Simple Paragraph

- Organizes related sentences
- Writes short paragraph on one subject
- Spells phonetically but somewhat consistently
- Writes short letters, such as thank-you notes

Stage Six: Beginning Story Writing

- Composes short narrative with simple sentences
- Uses many combining words, such as "and" or "but"
- Shows inconsistent capitalization and punctuation
- Uses standard spelling for some words

Stage Seven: Expanded Story Writing

- Writes stronger sentences with fewer connecting words
- Writes longer stories
- Uses more descriptions, especially colors
- Composes stories with a beginning, a middle, and an end
- Expands sentences to include compound and/or complex sentences
- Improves capitalization skills
- Uses more correct end punctuation

Stage Eight: Progressive Writing Skills

- Expands sentence patterns to include stronger adjectives, adverbs, phrases (prepositional, adverbial)
- Expands ability to use mechanics correctly to include initial capitalization, end punctuation, commas in a series, quotation marks for dialogue, and more correct spelling
- Uses correct paragraph structure: topic sentence, 3 details, concluding sentence
- Writes descriptive, expository, narrative, and persuasive paragraphs
- Edits own work for: overuse of "lazy" words, content, sentence structure (run-ons, fragments), paragraph structure, transitions (first, last)

Stage Nine: Advanced Writing Skills

- Combines two or more paragraphs with appropriate transitions
- Writes stronger introduction and conclusion
- Understands and uses literary devices: simile, metaphor, exaggeration, alliteration
- Expands story writing to show understanding of plot, conflict, suspense, setting, and characterization
- Expands self-editing skills to include: punctuation, spelling, grammar, tense, and voice
- Writes to inform: expository essays, book reports, news articles, letters
- Writes to express self and entertain others: short stories, poetry, drama, diaries
- Writing demonstrates understanding of cause/effect, problem solving, sequencing, comparison/contrast, summaries, generalization, and types of narration
- Writes research paper demonstrating ability to develop and use bibliography, take notes, outline, and use parenthetical citations

For student writing samples, refer to Student Work 1, pp. 118-119.

notes

notes

Journaling and Letter Writing

Overview

The road to becoming a good writer is paved by simply writing. A teacher's goal is to help students master writing skills painlessly. Journaling is a wonderful start. By keeping a journal, children can grow in expression and communication, as well as discover some surprising things about themselves through writing.

The most successful way to approach journaling is simply to expect students to write daily. Students keep their journals in a notebook. Upon entering the classroom each day, they find an assignment on the board. This routine proves to be a wonderful management technique. By adhering to this schedule, the teacher eliminates much potentially wasted time. The students enter the classroom, put things away, sharpen their pencils, and quickly get to work on their daily journals.

Evaluation of journal work is left to the discretion of the teacher. Allow mistakes and much freedom as students explore writing through this avenue. Expect more fine-tuned products from assignments completed in the other content areas.

Grade on participation. A check or comment at the top of each entry shows you actually read their efforts and provides a positive incentive for students. If a student feels an entry is too personal for even the teacher to read, (s)he places a paper clip on the top of the page. Check only to see that the assignment has been completed.

Children often formulate their ideas for stories and journal entries from home experiences. Be careful not to analyze children's backgrounds from either their stories or their journal entries. Children have vivid imaginations; accept their writing as products of that imagination.

Parental questions regarding privacy issues in journal writing occasionally surface. Teachers may also have concerns regarding this matter. If you feel uneasy about privacy issues, monitor your journal prompts carefully. Journal writing is meant to allow children to experience the pure joy and freedom of writing. A wide variety of ideas leads to "fun" writing and does not intrude upon a child's privacy.

Students benefit from keeping a subject-related journal in addition to a personal journal. Incorporate as many other content areas as possible into subject-related journal writing. For example, have students record various assignments, their results, and personal reactions to the assignments.

Beginning a Reading Log

A reading log, where students record questions, feelings, and other responses to reading assignments, can become either part of journal writing or a separate activity. After reading a passage aloud, have students respond to questions, such as: What did you see ... taste ... hear ... smell ... as I was reading? What do you think is about to happen?

After discussing an assignment, ask students to address questions such as: Why do you think (a character) reacted this way? What does the character's reaction reveal about him/her? How would you feel in a similar situation?

Extend the reading log to include student analysis of point of view, setting, themes, characterization, and plot. Begin with a one-paragraph assignment. By midyear, students in grades 4-6 should be expected to write at least one page per entry.

Variation: Have students create a poem about the story or book. For poetry forms, refer to Student Handout 5, pp. 112-114.

Journal Ideas

Beginning of School

1. My favorite/worst part of the summer was....

2. The way I have changed as a person over the last year is....

3. Describe how you felt the first day of school.

4. I was most excited about this class because....

5. The class goals I have set for myself this year are....

6. With regard to my friends, this year I hope to....

7. My only regret about this summer is....

8. If the principal asked me to give three suggestions to improve our school, they would be....

Holidays and Special Events

October

1. You are Columbus trying to convince the king and queen of Spain to finance your trip to India. List the benefits Spain would receive from this endeavor.

2. Describe your costume for the Harvest/Halloween Festival.

3. Describe a time in your life when you were paralyzed with fear.

November/December

1. What are you most thankful for this Thanksgiving season?

2. What are some of your favorite holiday activities?

3. What are some of the stresses and pressures associated with family gatherings? What would you say/do to help eliminate these problems?

4. Which holiday is your favorite? Why?

5. What holiday traditions do you plan to continue when you grow up?

6. The best part of my vacation was....

7. The worst part of my vacation was....

8. You are in charge of evaluating the latest toys on the market. What is your criteria?

Spring

1. You are running for a school office. Respond to the following questions: What are your goals? What would you do to improve your school? How would you resolve specific problems at your school (e.g., poor attitudes, unruly behavior in the halls, disorganized cafeteria situation)?

2. Design a coat of arms for your school. Complete these sentences: We think.... We wish.... We fear.... We like.... We ask.... We are.... Design an appropriate emblem to correlate with these ideas.

January

You are a slave on a Southern plantation. You receive word that you are being sold to another slave owner. Write a letter to your younger brother explaining why you must go. This letter should inform as well as console him.

Imagine a conversation between George Washington and Bill Clinton. Write the dialogue they might have if George Washington were transported to the White House today.

End of the Year

1. Your class has asked you to write a letter to be sealed in a time capsule and read on graduation night; describe your future appearance and thoughts.

2. My greatest accomplishment this year….

3. I plan to work on … this summer.

4. Describe what you see yourself doing ten years from now. How do you look?

5. What will the world be like ten years from now?

6. What is your most significant accomplishment?

7. Students at your school like a certain hairstyle. You secretly dislike it. Your best friend gets this hairstyle. What do you say and/or do?

8. Would you choose to be home-schooled, educated in a private school, or educated in a public school? What are your reasons?

General

1. Place a famous quote on the board. Have students write a response to the quote. Example: Patrick Henry's "Give me liberty or give me death."

2. Place a prompt on the board. Students enter class, settle at their desks, and begin to write. Examples:

   Today I feel….
   I get angry when….
   My idea of a great weekend is….
   I wish my parents knew….
   I would like to be….
   I often worry about….
   I wish I could….
   I look forward to….
   My only regret is….
   I wish my father….
   I wish my mother….
   Most brothers and sisters….
   I am at my best when….
   For me, studying….
   I need a raise in my allowance. I plan to convince my parents by….
   Someday I want to become….
   An ideal friend is someone who….
   The ideal teacher is someone who….
   If I could change one thing about the world, I would….

Letter Writing

Capitalize on students' desire to write notes to other students by establishing a "mail box" center with a container for each student. Occasionally, allow students a few minutes (possibly after lunch or recess) to write and deliver their notes. This and the following activities give students the practice they need to improve their letter-writing skills.

Have students:

1. Write thank-you letters to parents who assisted with class parties or other school events.

2. Write invitations to parents for school events.

3. Write letters to grandparents explaining what they want for Christmas. (For students who do not celebrate Christmas, write a letter to parent(s), describing a specific toy or gift and explaining why they want that particular item.)

4. Write a letter of appreciation to the principal for a special assembly or privilege. This can be a letter requesting a special event.

5. Write a letter of appreciation to the music or art teacher for a special presentation or display.

6. Write a note of appreciation to the custodian, bus driver, or school crossing guard.

7. Write a Valentine's letter to grandparents, an aunt, or an uncle.

8. Write a fan letter to a favorite musician or actor.

9. Join or start a pen pal program, either with students in another city or with students at another school in the same city.

10. Write letters to themselves. At the beginning of the school year, students list their desired accomplishments for the upcoming semester. During January, students list their New Year's resolutions. (Keep the letters in an envelope, and return them to students at the end of the year.)

11. Write a letter to a favorite pet or a letter to parents explaining why they want a pet.

12. Write a letter of encouragement or apology.

13. Write a letter to parents explaining grades on a report card.

14. Write a letter to students just starting kindergarten explaining how to "survive" in school.

15. After reading a story, write a letter from one character to another explaining a particular situation. Or, write a letter from a character in one story to someone in another story.

16. Write a letter to the author of a book expressing feelings about the book. Consider mailing the letter to the publishing company.

17. Write a letter to the school librarian recommending a book for other students to read.

notes

Developing a Writing Program

Directives

1. Children learn to write by writing. Make assignments interesting, purposeful, and meaningful. Rather than focusing on exercises about "how to write," teach children to write what they see and feel. Consider developing individual spelling lists based on misspelled words in a student's writing.

2. Writing is a developmental process. For beginning writers, concentrate primarily on content. Children cannot learn to express themselves and master mechanics simultaneously.

3. Respond to the content with positive comments. Don't return a paper that is "bleeding to death." Nothing stifles early writing endeavors as much as a teacher's disapproval.

4. Gradually focus on mechanics and form. For example, concentrate on one or two areas of mechanics in a specific assignment. Give instructions before students begin the assignment, then give two grades: one for content and one for mechanics.

5. Accept children at their individual developmental levels. Read and comment on each student's paper accordingly. Set up student/teacher conferences that will enable you to offer suggestions and encouragement. In addition, have students plan a student/parent conference. Each student plans and conducts the conference. Students explain to parents the format and requirements for their sample writing assignments. Have parent(s) sign a conference sheet for the student's folder stating that the child has clearly explained the writing process.

6. Consider establishing peer response groups. Suggestions for establishing and monitoring these groups can be found on the following pages.

7. Allow students to write occasionally just for the fun of writing. This can be accomplished through journaling or letter writing.

8. Display students' papers in various stages of the process (brainstorming, rough draft), as well as finished products. Include sample work from all students, not just the neat, correct papers.

Peer Response Groups

Points to consider before having students work in peer response groups:

1. Students must always list at least one strength.

2. Students will respond to no more than one or two skills at a time.

3. Change the response form to indicate the selected skill(s) and the specific target areas (e.g., clear beginning, middle, ending; punctuation; spelling; capitalization; sentence structure; overuse of "lazy" words). For sample evaluation forms, refer to Student Handouts 1 & 2, pp. 108-109.

Suggested target areas for peer comments:

1. Tell what you liked best about the paper.

2. List nouns, verbs, adjectives, and adverbs.

3. Was anything about the story unclear to you?

4. Summarize the story in one sentence.

5. Rewrite unclear sentences.

Guidelines

1. Assign students to groups of three or four. Choose students with different personality types: the "leader," the "talker," the "quiet one." Keep the same groups for several assignments, unless the students have obvious difficulty working together.

2. Appoint a different group leader each time the group works together. Choose the leader based on objective criteria, such as the student with the closest birth date or the student wearing a specific color.

3. Give a group grade. Suggested criteria for group grade (see note below):

   A. Each group starts the activity with 100 points.

   B. Deduct 10 points for each infraction of the following rules.

   - Only the leader may ask the teacher a question.
   - Students must remain on task (no visiting).
   - Discussion should be confined to within their own group.
   - Students should refrain from arguing.

An easy method for keeping track of a group's score is to use numbered cups containing 10 popsicle sticks or strips of paper. Number cups to correspond with groups. Remove one stick or strip from the group's cup each time an infraction of the rules occurs.

Note: A standard policy for group interaction creates a workable group atmosphere and employs positive "peer pressure" to encourage participating students to conform to the guidelines. As a result, students learn to work together and to depend on each other, rather than on the teacher.

4. Format:

   A. Before beginning group work, suggest that student authors list areas where they want a group response (e.g., content or sentence structure).

   B. Direct students to take turns reading papers aloud to the group; group members may offer positive comments.

   C. Have each student read the papers; write specific comments regarding content, clarity, and mechanics; and complete their evaluation sheets. Remind students that general comments such as "I liked it" will not help the author.

notes

Writing Assignments

Types of Writing

The first part of this section explains different types of writing: descriptive, narrative, expository, persuasive. The second part includes classroom activities and assignments.

Descriptive Writing

Descriptive writing describes something clearly for the reader. The mental picture created may be of a person, place, thing, event, or experience. Descriptive writing allows the reader to see, hear, feel, taste, and/or smell what the author is describing. Often, this is only part of a longer piece of writing.

Teach students to describe the main object of a picture from top to bottom or from left to right and to describe the other parts last. Encourage students to use strong, dynamic adjectives. Refer to word lists for ideas. Develop creative passages to describe story settings and enhance characterizations. Stress that all writing must have a beginning and an ending; for example, begin with "This picture shows…." and end with "This is an unusual picture." Descriptive writing can also take the form of a story about the picture.

Narrative Writing

Narrative writing speaks to the reader, telling a story through a series of events. The events are usually arranged in chronological order. This account may be real or imaginary and may range from a short, simple narrative to a longer story. The author should use descriptive detail to explain the material.

Most children enjoy storytelling about real or imaginary events. The teacher's task is to guide them as they learn to put these stories on paper. Begin with a few sentences, which the student can dictate to the teacher or write with parental help at home.

Two forms of narration include *simple narrative* and *narrative with plot*. The simple narrative reports event(s) and is usually chronological and informative, such as a newspaper's account of an accident. The narrative with plot is less often chronological, written to fit a type of story, and to entertain.

Persuasive Writing

Persuasive writing attempts to persuade the reader to believe an opinion. A good persuasive paper includes convincing reasons to support the author's opinion. Advertisements and editorials are good examples of persuasive writing.

Expository Writing

Expository writing gives information or explains facts and ideas. This type of writing explains how to do something, what something means, why it is important, how it works, and/or when and where it occurs. Expository writing also includes comparison/contrast writing.

Patterns for comparison/contrast writing:

1. Divided pattern: Write everything about A, then write everything about B. Consider A as one topic, B as a separate topic. The introduction and conclusion state both topics. Outline:

   I. Introduction
   II. Topic 1
   III. Topic 2
   IV. Conclusion

2. Alternating Pattern: Write comparisons of the two topics in one section. Write contrasts of topics. The introduction and conclusion address both topics. Outline:

   I. Introduction
   II. Similarities
   III. Differences
   IV. Conclusion

3. Alternating pattern 2: Broad aspects of comparison or contrast are the topics. Subjects are handled alternately under each subtopic. Outline:

   I. Introduction
   II.   a. Comparison
         b. Contrast
   III. a. Comparison
         b. Contrast
   IV. Conclusion

The Writing Process

Suggestions for all types of writing:

Demonstrate a variety of brainstorming methods (outlining, mapping, clustering, webbing, story mapping, listing–defined below); students write sentences, paragraphs, or stories. Length and degree of difficulty should depend on grade level.

Students use one of the following brainstorming methods (e.g., outlining) to plan their piece. Students revise, then write the final copy. Allow time for students to practice all methods to determine which they prefer.

Outlining: Organize the subject matter into main topic and related subtopics.

Listing: Make a list of characters and events to organize ideas in a logical way.

Story Map: Draw a series of boxes (similar to a comic strip). In the first box, tell who the story is about and where and when it happened. In the other boxes, list events (or problems) in the story; in the last box, give the resolution of the story.

> Variation: In a box on the upper left side, list who the story is about and where and when it happened. Draw a line to the right side and develop a step-by-step box diagram in which you list events (or problems) in sequential order. Draw a line back to a box on the lower left side in which you state the resolution of the story.

Clustering: Put the main idea in a center square. Draw circles branching out above and below the center to the left and right. Place subordinating ideas in these circles. This gives students a logical pattern to follow.

Webbing: Place a box containing the centralized concept (title) in the center of the page. Draw long lines branching out in four directions; place the main ideas on these lines. Draw smaller lines branching out from each long line; place the ideas connected to the main ideas on these lines.

Story Pyramid: Plan a story using a pyramid form.

```
              1_____
            2_____ _____
          3_____ _____ _____
        4_____ _____ _____ _____
      5_____ _____ _____ _____ _____
    6_____ _____ _____ _____ _____ _____
```

Directions: Students write the following on the lines indicated.

Line 1: Name of the main character

Line 2: Two words that describe the main character

Line 3: Three words that tell where and when the story takes place (setting)

Line 4: Four words that describe the setting

Line 5: Five words that tell the most important thing that happens (climax)

Line 6: Six words that tell how the story ends

Preparatory Writing

Preparatory Writing

1. Have students list their favorite places to eat, vacation, and shop. Students choose one and free-write for ten minutes about this place: where it is, what they see there, why they like it, and one experience they had there.

2. Students analyze paper:

    A. Circle all nouns; add adjectives to at least three.

    B. Place brackets around the word "thing" any time it appears; replace with the name of the "thing."

    C. Place a box around these words: it, its, these, those, this, that; replace with the word to which the pronoun refers.

    D. Cross out the word "there" when it begins a sentence. Rewrite the sentence, placing the subject of the sentence first.

    E. Underline sentences that contain "you" or "your." Rewrite sentences using either the person's name or the third person pronoun.

    F. Rewrite the paper.

Descriptive Writing

Objective:

- To demonstrate an understanding of descriptive writing by writing a paragraph (or short story) that appeals to the five senses

Focus Activity:

Discuss sensory experiences with students. Have students describe things they have tasted, smelled, seen, touched, or heard throughout the day. Together, develop lists of tasting, smelling, seeing, touching, and hearing words. Display lists for reference.

Process:

Discuss descriptive writing. Show students a picture and read a descriptive paragraph about it. Point out the importance of describing things in a set pattern (e.g., top to bottom; left to right). Select a common experience (e.g., lunch time) and develop a classroom paragraph.

Assignment:

Students write a paragraph that helps the reader smell and taste a favorite meal, see an unusual person, hear the sounds of the playground at recess, or feel the bark of a tree or other object. Illustrate. The degree of difficulty and length of descriptive writing should depend on grade level.

Extensions:

1. Students take an imaginary walk and write what they hear, see, smell, and touch. Illustrate.

2. Brainstorm and write on the board ideas for words that describe the sights, sounds, tastes, and smells of a day at the county or state fair. Have students write their experiences and feelings during a day at the fair, either as a class activity or individually. This activity works well for writing about holiday dinners, a visit to the circus or zoo, or any special experience.

3. Place several objects in small paper bags. Give one bag to each student. Tell students to leave the object in the bag and observe secretly and silently. Students write a description of their object and read it to the class; other students draw the object as they visualize it. Suggested objects: feather, peanut, sea shell, hair bow, shoelace, baby rattle, teething ring, eyelash curler, round hair brush, baby fork, cocoon, rubber band, button, toothpick, screw, tube of lip balm, battery.

4. Distribute pictures of a variety of animals or people to students and have them write a description of their pictures. Display pictures around the room. Take up and redistribute descriptive papers. Students match descriptive papers to pictures.

5. Students describe their neighborhood, telling what is pleasing and/or displeasing to them. Include physical characteristics, types of people, and descriptions of houses, landscapes, and vehicles.

6. Students explain how cotton candy feels, smells, and tastes.

7. Students explain the taste, smell, and appearance of a hot dog or a slice of pizza to a visitor from outer space.

8. Students look through magazines and list ten descriptive words. Students exchange lists with a partner and write a story using words from partner's list.

9. Distribute copies of a paragraph written with bland adjectives. Have students replace weak words with strong descriptive words.

10. Students write descriptions of an unusual person or place and read them to the class; other students sketch what they picture as the descriptions are read.

11. Have students "step outside" themselves and write a paragraph describing themselves as individuals.

12. Show students a picture of an old house. Discuss what is visible. Have students describe the house to provide a complete picture for the reader. Students create a setting for a mystery or an adventure story.

Narrative Writing

Objective:

- To write a selection which demonstrates an understanding of narrative writing style

Focus Activity:

Have students share an experience, such as a trip to the doctor, a visit with grandparents, or a vacation.

Process:

Discuss narrative writing. Guide students to understand that narratives usually follow a sequential pattern. Select a recent event in which the class participated. Outline steps explaining the experience.

The following suggestions will help students improve their narrative writing.

- Write in a "real" voice as if events are actually happening. Be expressive and write clearly and concisely.
- Understand the audience for which the writing is intended (teacher, peers, parents).
- Begin with a strong lead and end with a strong conclusion.
- Use variety, including surprise twists. Search for imaginative ways to say something ordinary (e.g., dialogue).
- Use enough detail to make the narrative interesting but not so much that it becomes confusing.

Assignments:

1. Students write a narrative about an event in their lives. The level of difficulty and the length should depend on grade level. Stress using vivid words to convey ideas and the importance of a strong beginning and ending.

2. Students write a narrative about an imaginary trip they would like to take.

3. Students write a narrative about something interesting that has happened to them on the way to or from school. They can also make a map of the route from home to school.

Extensions:

1. Students select an entry from their journals and rewrite it as a narrative.

2. Students use one of these story starters as the first line of their narrative:

   I sit at the keyboard.... (perhaps first recital)
   The music begins for my first dance....
   I stand at the balance beam....
   My first game began....
   The ball flew straight toward me....
   We were in our last inning, two outs, one point behind....

   Variation: Bake cupcakes with a strip of paper inside, each one giving the first line of a narrative.

3. Students write a narrative about a big mistake, holiday memories, getting lost, running away, being alone, or feeling homesick.

4. Students write a narrative about a hobby or collection, telling how this interest began, the length of time involved, etc. Have students bring a sample of their hobby or collection from home to show the class as they read their narratives.

Expository Writing

Objective:

- To demonstrate an understanding of expository writing by writing a step-by-step procedure

Focus Activity:

Have an object hidden in the classroom. Give students clues to its hiding place until someone finds it.

Process:

Discuss expository writing. Explain that someone found the hidden object by following the step-by-step clues.

Assignments:

1. Each student imagines (s)he has hidden something valuable and writes step-by-step directions for finding the object, starting at a selected point. Illustrate with a treasure map.

2. Students write a step-by-step procedure for making something, such as a paper airplane.

3. Students prepare a step-by-step sentence outline for the events in "Jack and the Beanstalk."

4. Students plan a step-by-step shopping trip to buy school clothes.

5. Write an expository paper explaining the causes of acid rain or another natural phenomena, such as tornadoes.

Collaborative Assignments

The class develops a guidebook for their school. Students are assigned (in small groups) to interview school personnel (principal, nurse, librarian, custodian) and report guidelines for different departments, school disciplinary procedures, and basic school rules to the class. Make prior arrangements with personnel and help students develop a list of questions. Compile information and develop a student handbook. Students illustrate different sections; teacher or a student can type information. Duplicate and distribute to new students. This assignment promotes cohesiveness between students, pride in their school, and the ability to write collaboratively.

Extensions:

1. Students write the procedure for a science experiment, or directions for teaching a toddler to walk or a child to ride a bicycle.

2. Students design the perfect play area (room at home, classroom), explaining why certain objects should be included.

3. Students plan a perfect party from beginning to end, listing the occasion, location, guests, and menu. This is a good collaborative assignment for small groups.

4. Compare kinds of music, city living vs. country living, types of friends.

5. Compare a book with its movie version.

6. Write a paper explaining the proper way to care for a pet. Include the things needed, steps to follow, problems that might occur, and ways to improve the process. The planning sheet on p. 110 (Student Handout 3) works well for this type of assignment.

Persuasive Writing

Objective:

- To write a selection which demonstrates an understanding of persuasive writing techniques

Focus Activity:

1. Display ads from magazines, especially those designed to appeal to children of the age group with which you are working. Ask students which products they would buy and why. Discuss current television advertisements that appeal to children.

2. Bring a toy that looked or sounded wonderful when it was advertised but broke the first time it was used. Ask students when they have had a similar experience. This is an excellent lesson on consumerism and is a useful tool for teaching discernment and smart shopping.

Process:

Discuss how print and television advertisements are designed to persuade the reader to buy a particular product. Point out persuasive words (biggest, best, etc.). Brainstorm and list words that are used in advertising directed at children.

Variation: Discuss persuasive techniques students use with parents (or others) to gain permission for something. Point out the importance of at least three positive points and support for each point. Practice writing a classroom letter to the principal in which students ask for special permission for a field trip.

Assignments:

1. Show students a variety of products (pictures or actual objects) that are marketed for their age group. As a classroom activity or individually, have students develop an advertisement (TV or radio commercial, and/or newspaper or magazine ad) for one product. Include promotional rationale and advertising techniques.

2. Write a public service announcement (PSA) to convey a message to parents or the public about something that concerns students. This should be 15-60 seconds long when read. Consider the following points:

   • target audience
   • problem or opportunity PSA will address
   • desired audience response
   • information needed to get audience response.

3. Design a bumper sticker that conveys a persuasive message.

Extensions:

1. Write a letter to the school principal asking for something such as a longer lunch hour.

2. Write a letter to parents or guardians requesting permission to attend an event or to gain extended privileges.

3. Each student chooses a problem someone his or her age might have. Pretend a friend has this problem. Write a letter persuading the friend to seek help.

4. Students write advertising jingles and set them to music (collaborative or individual assignment).

5. Write a letter to the school board requesting permission for girls to participate in football.

notes

A Closer Look at Stories

Foreword

Story writing is one of the core components of an elementary creative writing syllabus. Most students love listening to stories, and have a wealth of ideas that can be developed into stories.

This unit includes a wide variety of suggestions for story writing. It also introduces a glossary of fundamental words. Together, these basic concepts will serve as a building block for more advanced writing. Use the glossary as needed for different grade levels. Focus on the concepts and not the words.

The assignments can be adapted for different grade levels. Younger students can write collaborative classroom stories. The expected length and level of difficulty can also be varied.

Glossary*

Protagonist: the main character

Antagonist: the character in opposition to the protagonist; can be another person, nature, or himself/herself

Point of View: first person narration (uses I, me, my, we, our, us); third person (uses he, she, they, them)

Setting: place and time period of story

Plot: sequence of events in story

Plot Structure:

1. Exposition: an introduction to the main characters, primary setting, and situations of the story
2. Rising Action: the events and complications that lead to an important dramatic point in the story
3. Climax: the point of greatest interest and emotional involvement in the story; turning point
4. Falling Action: the events that develop from the climax and lead to the conclusion
5. Denouement: the final outcome of the story; also called the resolution

Conflict: problems or conflict between protagonist and antagonist

Dialogue: conversation between two or more people

Foreshadowing: an event that hints at something that will happen later

Mood: emotional feeling of the story

* Teacher Reference

Story Writing

Objective:

- To help students develop their ideas into a logically organized story that incorporates descriptive and narrative writing

Focus Activities:

For each story-writing assignment, focus on the type of story you want children to write.

1. Have students recall a favorite story from early childhood, tell why it was special, and list specific things they remember about the story.

2. Discuss types of stories (mystery, adventure, travel, fantasy).

Process:

Discuss the importance of planning. Model a planning design (see Writing Process section, page 39) and use a story idea, such as an adventure in an underground cave or a story students have recently read, to demonstrate how a story takes shape during the planning stage.

Have students select a type of planning design for their story. Check planning stage.

Assignments:

This section includes a variety of ideas to help students begin writing stories. Story starters and suggested titles are listed for travel, fantasy, mystery, and adventure stories.

Travel Story

1. You are a traveler in outer space and have just arrived on Mars. Explain how you got there and what you found when you arrived.

2. You are an astronaut on a spaceship. You have just landed on the moon and have met the "Man in the Moon." Write a story about this man and your experiences while on the moon.

3. Using a road map, plan a trip that takes you 500 miles from home (modify distance for younger students). Tell about your adventures on the trip. Include the number of days you will travel, the stops you will make, and what you will see along the way. This is an interesting assignment for teacher and students to do together.

Fantasy Story

1. Plan a city in space (or on the ocean floor). Write a story about your life in this city. Illustrate.

2. Pretend you are a famous player of your favorite sport. Tell the story of an important game from your point of view.

3. Write a story about a day in the life of … (feather, seashell–before and after the death of inhabitant, teething ring, rubber band, toothpick, cocoon, egg about to hatch, rhinoceros).

4. Write a tall tale. Design and illustrate a poster about the tale.

5. Rewrite a fairy tale or nursery rhyme, changing the setting to a contemporary one.

    Variation: Rewrite a fairy tale as a poem.

Mystery Story

1. Write a story about "The Case of the Missing ... (Sneaker, Teacher, Class)."

2. Your teacher will read "Little Miss Muffet." Discuss Miss Muffet's reaction to the spider. Draw a picture of something you're afraid of and write a mystery story about the picture (who is afraid, why, what happens).

Story Starters:

Something was wrong, terribly wrong.
Someone screamed my name.
I stuck my hand in the box and pulled out....
I entered the haunted house and....
The fear started when....
We waited anxiously....
The police found only one clue....
The note said, "We are watching you."
Suddenly, the lights went out.

Adventure Story

Suggested Titles:

- The Lion Who Couldn't Roar
- The Giraffe Who Had a Sore Throat
- The Day the School Bus Ran Backward
- The Magic Shoes
- The Day I Became Invisible
- Captured by Pirates
- The Day My Mom (or Dad) and I Switched Places

Additional Story Starters:

I started sliding down the hill....
Suddenly, I heard the rattle of a snake....
I heard a bear growl just outside our camper....
Gigantic footprints surrounded our tent....

Extension:

If possible, pair students from your class with students from junior high school or high school and have them write a story about or for each other. Older students can spend a class period with the children, then write and illustrate a story for them. To follow up, they can return to the classroom to read and present these stories to the younger children. With the assistance of their teacher, children can prepare a story and picture for the older students. This is an excellent learning experience for both groups (and their teachers!).

Writing Books

Objective:

Students will become authors by planning and writing a children's book

Focus Activity:

Have students bring a favorite book to class. In addition, have a variety of children's books available. Ask students which of the books they have read were their favorites and why. Discuss the importance of illustrations. Point out differences between picture books and other types of books. (1 day)

Process:

In groups of two or three, have students analyze some books, looking for the following:

- strong beginning (lead) and ending (conclusion)
- characterization (positive, negative)
- grade level (grade, age)
- vocabulary
- average number of sentences per page
- story development (strong throughout, strong usually, weak)
- interest level (high, average, low)
- cover, illustrations

To analyze picture books:

- cover
- number of words/number of illustrations
- size of illustrations
- size of words
- simplicity of words and sentences

Report on analysis to class (2 days).

Assignments:

Students write and illustrate a book. This can be done individually, with a partner, or in small groups. Distribute planning sheets (Student Handout 4, p. 111).

The complete book should include:

- illustrated text
- title page with names of author(s)
- story with illustrations
- about the author(s)

Laminate covers of books. If possible, arrange to have students' books bound. Often, a book binder is available in the curriculum office. If this is not feasible, laminate covers and put together with brads.

Extensions:

1. Students write and illustrate a book for younger children. This can be an original story or a rewritten play, a book, or a Bible story. If possible, arrange for them to read their stories to the appropriate age group.

2. Students create a picture alphabet book for younger children. Illustrations should be creative and the text should include a sentence or two to fit the picture.

3. Students write a "Grandparents" book. Interview a grandparent and write a book about his/her experiences. Include photographs and illustrations.

4. Students write and illustrate a book with creative uses of homonyms (dear, deer) and/or homographs (bat, bat). Examples:

   The *blue* wind *blew* my kite away. (homonym)
   The *bass* fish had a *bass* voice. (homograph)
   The *chow* (breed of dog) ate his *chow* (food). (homonym/homograph)

After students complete their books, have them advertise by making posters for their books. Place these around the room. Give students special recognition for their work by planning an authors' party or a book fair. Consider having this in the library or cafeteria (possibly with refreshments). For the authors' party, invite parents, administrators, and photographers from the yearbook or local newspaper. Have students at a table with their books to show their work and answer questions. For a book fair, invite teachers and students from other grades to see the finished products. This project also makes an excellent display for open house.

Autobiographical Writing

Objective:

- To write an autobiography

Focus Activity:

Display photos of yourself and students on the bulletin board. Relate an early memory; then ask students to tell something about themselves, including one or two early memories. Share and discuss autobiographies with students (especially some with pictures).

Process:

Discuss why people write stories about themselves. Read portions of an autobiography. Point out to students that stories about themselves are important to others. Discuss important things they might include (names of parents, where they were born, an early memory, events related to them by someone else).

Discuss how to write an autobiography: chronologically or as a flashback from present; include special memories; can be imaginary interview with self (question/answer); can be written as a letter to someone; can include interview with partner(s), sibling(s), or others.

Assignment:

Each student prepares an illustrated autobiography. Include pictures that show different stages of his/her life. Design a cover with a current picture of the student and illustrations that show something about his/her interests. (Length and difficulty will depend on grade level.)

Extensions:

Have students:

1. Write a chapter of their autobiography, such as a time that was especially meaningful.

2. Write an autobiography of selected scenes, such as earliest memories, followed by memories at two-year intervals.

3. Write about memories from each summer vacation, special holiday, or school year.

4. Write a series of adventures from their lives that involve riding (e.g., stroller, tricycle, bicycle, skates).

5. Write memories of special people in their lives, telling who they are and giving one special memory about each one.

Characterizations

Objective:

- To understand what characterization means and to write a characterization that shows the physical and mental qualities of a person

Focus Activity:

Display pictures of people with different physical characteristics and different emotions (include babies' pictures). Discuss what the picture reveals about the person. Talk about expressions on the babies' faces and have students predict the type of personality the baby will develop.

Process:

Complete one or more.

1. Distribute photocopies of a selected tee-shirt outline. Students create a design that shows their interests and personality.

2. Choose a classroom model, perhaps the child with the nearest birthday. Talk about the child's physical characteristics and personality, always stressing positive points.

3. Divide the class into groups of four or five students. Distribute adhesive note paper. Have each student in the group write a comment on appearance or personality about each group member (must be positive) and stick the note on the recipient's back. Students retrieve notes from their backs and read comments. Discuss how we view other people.

Assignments:

Classroom or group assignments:

1. Choose someone all the children know (music or art teacher, nurse, principal, etc.).

2. Brainstorm with students and list the person's characteristics on the board under categories such as appearance, personality, and type of job.

3. Develop a classroom characterization of the person.

4. Have each child draw a picture of the subject. Invite recipient to the classroom and present him/her with children's pictures and the characterization.

Individual assignments:

1. Each student chooses a special person and writes a characterization of that person. Include unique physical and personality characteristics of the selected person. This would make a nice gift.

2. Students write their characterizations in first-person format (for example, "I Am a Mother" or "I Am a Teacher").

3. While reading a book (individually or as a class), students develop a "cast of characters" chart for the primary two or three characters. As the story progresses, students fill in information about the characters' physical and personality traits. Write a characterization of a character from the book. Tell what (s)he is like at the beginning of the book, how (s)he changes throughout the story (including what caused the changes), and what (s)he is like at the end of the book.

notes

A Closer Look at Poetry

Poetry Writing

Objectives:

- To write a series of formula poems and a variety of free verse or rhyming poems

- To demonstrate an understanding of poetic devices, including alliteration, onomatopoeia, metaphor, simile, and rhyming couplets

- To develop an illustrated poetry notebook

Focus Activity:

Have a student recite the poem "Roses Are Red." Ask students to recall other versions they have heard. Have students share rhymes (jump rope rhymes, folk rhymes).

Process:

1. Read a favorite poem and discuss its meaning (vary according to age level). Talk about rhyming and non-rhyming poems.

2. Distribute poetry forms (Student Handout 5, pp. 112-114) and copies of poetry writing (Student Work 2, pp. 120-124). Model types of poems, adjusting for grade level. Include formula poems and examples of poetic devices such as alliteration and onomatopoeia.

Poetry Notebook

Assignments:

Students write a series of poems and place them in a self-designed poetry notebook (Student Handout 6, p. 115).

Materials

Distribute photocopied handouts:

- pattern for leaf for the Poet Tree
- pattern for stepping stones
- patterns for various animals
- pictures: nature, landscape (mountains, valleys, meadows), vehicles

Suggestions for displaying students' poems:

Poet Tree: Decorate a bulletin board to look like a tree with branches. Each student writes his/her haiku or cinquain on the outline of a leaf. These "leaves" become leaves on the branches of the tree.

Stepping Stones: Students write poems (any type) on the outline of a stepping stone. Then, arrange "stones" so they lead to or across a brook sketched on the bulletin board. Students write poems on stepping stones to represent memories at different age levels. These can be placed on a student's growth chart.

Pet Store: Students write poems about their pets on the pattern picturing the corresponding animal. Place these poems in a "pet store" sketched on the bulletin board, or hang them on the walls of a cardboard pet store.

Assignment:

Have students write a class rap. This can be done in groups or with the entire class collaborating with the teacher. Example:

Mrs. Gunter's Class Rule Rap*

Here are the rules for Gunter's Gators:
We're a class of non-haters.

Always be considerate and kind
And you'll find out that you'll do fine.

Be alert and pay attention
Or you'll be in in-school suspension.

Make sure your language is polite;
You'll make friends and never fight.

Treat others as you'd like to be treated,
Or in time-out you'll be seated.

Don't talk when someone else is talking,
Or to the office you'll be walking.

This is the end of our class rhyme.
We've got to go; we're out of time.

* Written by fourth-grade students of Pat (Gunter) Benson, Temple, Texas.

notes

notes

Reading and Writing Connection

Assignments

Objectives:

- To understand the correlation between reading and writing

- To write a creative discourse that correlates with a book

Students understand and relate to a book better when they write a creative response to it or write their own imaginary story. This section includes brief synopses of a wide variety of books, each with a corresponding writing assignment.

Focus Activities:

Employ a variety of focus activities to introduce the book:

1. Read the first few paragraphs; ask students what they think the book is about.

2. Look at the cover; discuss what the book might be about based on the pictures on the cover.

3. Read a selected portion about the main character; discuss what might happen to him/her in the book.

Process:

Students or teacher read the book. Discuss one or more components of the book: plot, characterization, setting.

Assignments:

An assignment accompanies each synopsis on the following pages.

Baseball Saved Us by Ken Mochizuki (Santa Monica, CA: Lee & Low Books, Inc., 1993) Shorty and his family, along with thousands of other Japanese-Americans, are forced to relocate from their home to a Japanese-American internment camp during World War II after the attack on Pearl Harbor. Fighting the heat, dust, and freezing cold nights of the desert, Shorty and the others at the camp need something to look forward to, even if only for nine innings. So they build a playing field. Shorty soon finds that he is playing not only to win, but also to gain dignity and self-respect as well. **Assignment**: How do you react when someone yells at you or tells you that you can't achieve a certain goal? Have you ever been singled out and made fun of because of your race, gender, physical appearance, or other factors? Write a narrative that explains your reaction to criticism from others.

Birthday Surprises edited by Johanna Hurwitz (New York: Morrow Junior Books, 1995) Ten popular children's authors wrote stories based on the premise of receiving a beautifully wrapped package that turned out to be empty. **Assignment**: (This assignment is more effective when students write their stories before reading the book.) Teacher brings a beautifully wrapped, empty package to class. Unwrap it and have children write a story that tells about someone who opens a package like this. Compare their stories with the stories in the book.

Please see these selections which are part of the above book:

Hattie's Birthday Box by Pam Conrad
No Such Thing by Ann M Martin
Birthday Box by Jane Yolen
Victor by James Home
Promises by Ellen Conford

Digging Up Dinosaurs by Aliki (New York: HarperCollins Children's Books, 1988) This book answers questions about the Ignanodon, Apatosaurus, and Tyrannosaurus. Where did these enormous skeletons come from? How did they get inside museums? Today, teams of experts work together to dig dinosaur fossils out of the ground and then put together skeletons that look just like the dinosaurs of millions of years ago. **Assignment**: Answer the following questions in an expository essay: Have you ever been to see a huge dinosaur exhibit? Would you be interested in searching for fossils? On which part of the team would you want to be included? Why? How do paleontologist and geologist differ?

Donald and the Fish that Walked by Edward R. Ricciuti (New York: HarperCollins Children's Books, 1974) Donald's dog, Sam, finds a pink fish with eyes like shiny stones. But this is no ordinary fish. It walks. This true event took place in Florida in March of 1967. The *Clarias batrachus* arrived from South Asia. The fish were two feet long, with venomous spines and a special set of organs that allowed them to breathe air. Their arrival upset the balance of nature. They were finally killed by a cold spell. **Assignment**: Imagine you are in charge of the search for these fish and must decide how to preserve the balance of nature in Florida. In an expository essay, explain what you would do.

Fables by Arnold Lobel (New York: HarperCollins Children's Books, 1980) This is a collection of fables which can be used to teach many truths. **Assignment**: Have students write a one-page fable.

Gila Monsters Meet You at the Airport by Marjorie Weinman Sharmat (New York: Macmillan Publishers, 1980) This is a story about a child's anxieties and fears about moving from the East to the West. **Assignment**: Describe an experience that you feared at first, only to have it turn out much better than you could have imagined.

Helen Keller by Stewart and Polly Graff (New York: Dell Yearling, 1980) This is the story of Helen Keller. At six years old she is like a wild, frightened animal. She cannot see, hear, or speak. Then Anne Sullivan comes to stay. She traces letters, then words in Helen's hand until Helen understands this will be her way of communicating with others. Helen grows up and dedicates herself to helping others by teaching them what she learned from Anne Sullivan. **Assignment**: Write a short outline of major events in the story. Draw a comic strip or create a slide presentation that represents these main events. Write a caption for each picture.

Kate Shelley Bound by Legend by Robert D. San Souci (New York: Dial Books, 1995)
A terrible storm comes one summer night in 1881. A train wreck occurs near fifteen-year-old Kate's farm. Kate knows she must go for help and warn any incoming trains of danger ahead. Risking her life, she sets out through the dangerous night to find the survivors of the wreck. **Assignments**: 1. Explain what made Kate Shelley famous. 2. Name an important characteristic of Kate Shelley and explain how it caused her to choose her career. Did her life make the world a better place? Why or why not? Write a characterization of Kate Shelley.

Nettie Jo's Friends by Patricia C. McKissack (New York: Alfred A. Knopf, 1989) Nettie Jo is in search of a sewing needle. She must stitch Annie Mae a dress for the big wedding tomorrow. She takes time to help many others on her journey to find the needle, but none of the other friends treat her the same. Just when she is about to give up on the friends and the dress, someone shows up on her doorstep. **Assignment**: Write a short narrative answering the following questions: Have you ever been let down by a friend? Have you ever given up on a friendship? Why is friendship an important investment? Is it always worth it? How would you feel if you didn't have close friends?

Pink and Say by Patricia Polacco (New York: Putnam & Grosset Group, 1995) A young boy named Say is wounded in a fierce battle and left for dead in a pasture somewhere in Georgia. A black boy named Pink finds him. Pinkus is flying Union Colors like the wounded boy, so he picks him up from the field and takes him to where Moe Bay, his mother, lives. Moe Bay takes care of both boys. But they are Union Soldiers in Confederate Territory, and they are putting her in danger. They must find their troops again and rejoin them. They are scared and uncertain when the Confederate troops arrive. **Assignment**: Compare Pink and Say. How are they alike and different? Which one did you like the best and why?

Sami and the Time of the Troubles by Florence Parry Heide and Judith Heide Gilliland (New York: Clarion Books, 1992) Ten-year-old Sami lives in Beirut, the Capital of Lebanon. Until the middle of the twentieth century, Beirut was one of the most splendid cities in the world. Today it is a place of ruin and trouble. Sami and sister Leila are like children everywhere, but their lives are difficult because violence is the way differences are resolved in their country. **Assignment**: Compare/contrast your life and Sami's. How is your life different from Sami's? How is it the same? How would you react on the country's violent days? How do you like to resolve differences?

Stranded at Plymouth Plantation 1626 by Gary Bowen (New York: HarperCollins, 1995)
This is the story of the Sparrowhawks, which set sail October 12th from London to the destination of Jamestown, Virginia. On November 6th, the ship crashes onto the New England shore because of fog. Christopher Sears, a 13-year-old orphan, keeps a journal account of his first months in the New World while living with the Brewster family who arrived at Plymouth nearly six years earlier on the Mayflower. **Assignments**: 1. Explain why pioneers moved to new places and made new homes. Identify some of their hardships and how they overcame them. 2. Write a paragraph that describes the setting of this book. In a separate paragraph, answer these questions: Would you like to have lived in this time? Why or why not?

The Christmas Box by Richard Paul Evans (New York: Simon & Schuster, 1993) This is a story about a young family struggling to make it financially. Because of a bit of luck, they are able to lessen money stresses by living with a widow in her beautiful mansion. This experience is worth more than money. They learn the value of family, love, and life and come to understand the true spirit of Christmas. **Assignment**: Tell something tragic that happened to one of the characters in the story. Explain how it happened, the outcome of the experience, what the character learned from the experience, and how it changed the character.

The Sign of the Beaver by Elizabeth George Speare (New York: Dell Publishing, 1984) Twelve-year-old Matt is forced to learn to survive on his own after he is separated from his family. He is not prepared for an attack of swarming bees. He is rescued by an Indian chief and his grandson Attean. A friendship develops between Attean and Matt. Attean learns English while Matt becomes a skilled hunter. With no sign of the return of his family and winter near, the Beaver Tribe asks Matt to join them as they move north. Should Matt abandon all hope of finding his family and join them? **Assignment**: Write a characterization of Matt. How does he mature throughout the story? Explain what he is like at the beginning, the steps that cause him to mature, and what he is like at the end.

The Treasure Tree by John and Cindy Trent, Gary and Norma Smalley (Irving, TX: Word Kids, 1992) It's the biggest, best birthday party ever! Wise old owl gives each of four animal friends who share the same birthday a treasure map as a gift. The treasure they find at the end of their search is more than they imagined, and the lessons they learn along the way are priceless. On their adventure, they discover that their different personalities are some of the most precious treasures they have. **Assignment**: Compare a character from the story with yourself. Explain similarities/differences.

The True Princess by Angela Elwell Hunt (New York: Chariot Books, 1992) Hard times come upon a generous king and his only child. He is forced to go away to another kingdom and the child is hidden. During this time, the young princess grows. Through her struggles, she learns that true happiness comes from within, not from exterior things. **Assignment**: Write a paragraph that explains the feelings of one character at the beginning of the story, in the middle, and at the end. Explain circumstances that caused these feelings.

The Value of Truth and Trust—The Story of Cochise by Ann D. Johnson (Stamford, CT: Value Communication, 1977) This is a tale of a trustworthy person named Cochise. The story is based on actual events in his life. **Assignment**: Tell about Cochise's desire to be truthful and trustworthy. What caused him to feel this way? Did his feelings change in the book? Explain why and how.

Books to Read Aloud

Ramona the Pest by Beverly Cleary (New York: Dell Publishing, 1982)

Hank the Cowdog (a series) by John Erickson (Houston: Gulf Publishing)

Miracle at Clement's Pond by Patricia Pendergraft (New York: Putnam, 1987)

The Trouble with Secrets by Karen Johnson (Seattle, WA: Parenting Press, 1986)

The Legend of the Bluebonnet: An Old Tale of Texas by Tomie DePaola (New York: Putnam, 1983)

Little House on the Prairie (a series) by Laura Ingalls Wilder (New York: HarperCollins Children's Books, 1970s)

Amazing Grace by Mary Hoffman (New York: Dial Books, 1991)
The subject material in many Dial Books features high moral characteristics.

Madeline at Cooking School from a series by Ludwig Bemelamans (New York: Division of Penguin Books, 1958) This series is found in Viking Child Books and Puffin Books; both are divisions of Penguin Books.

Stellaluna by Janelle Cannon (New York: Harcourt Brace, 1993)

New American Girl Books

These books are from the American Girls Collection (Middleton, WI: Pleasant Co.)

Meet Felicity
Meet Kirstin
Meet Addy
Meet Molly
Meet Samantha

Movies with Character Building Emphasis

Babe—caring
Heidi—empathy and loyalty
The Secret Garden—self-reliance
Apollo 13—teamwork
A Little Princess—courage
American Panda—responsibility
An Indian in the Cupboard—responsibility

Additional Assignments

1. After reading a book about a mode of transportation, pretend you are a ... (tractor, train, airplane). Write a story about your life. This idea could also work with other inventions or animals.

2. Select a passage from a book that made you feel ... (sad, lonely, happy, fearful, excited, angry). Now write your own paragraph that makes someone else feel.... Use strong adjectives.

3. Make a time line to fit a particular book. Identify important events from the book on the time line.

4. Write a short sequel to a book.

5. Make a collage or scrapbook of pictures that relate to the book. Include original pictures and pictures from magazines or newspapers. If you make a scrapbook, put a caption under each picture that explains how it relates to the book.

6. Create a poem about a book.

7. Write a "reader response" to a book in your journal.

8. Rewrite a story; change the personality of a character and/or add a new character.

Book Report and Story Summary Ideas

1. Write a report or summary in poetry form.

2. Choose a character from the book. Compare/contrast this character with someone you know.

3. Describe the setting and tell how it is alike/different from where you live.

4. Rewrite in your own words one of the following:

   - the funniest incident
   - the most exciting or thrilling incident
   - the saddest incident
   - the scariest incident
   - the strangest or most unusual incident

5. Write your book report on a design that represents the book; for example, a report on *The Incredible Journey* (New York: Bantam Books, Inc., 1977) could be written on the sketch of a cat or dog.

6. List the main characters and write one descriptive sentence about each one.

7. Summarize a story in telegram form. (Make forms available to students.)

8. Write diary entries the main character might have written during important times.

9. Select one exciting section of the book and write it as a play.

Variation: Create a filmstrip presentation and show it to the class. Write and read an accompanying monologue about the book. Note: Teachers, you can prepare a blank filmstrip for students by soaking outdated filmstrips in a bleach mixture. Rinse in clear water and dry. Have available several transparency pens or permanent markers. Students can bring their own cassettes with background music and other sound effects.

notes

Short Assignments

Word Studies

Objectives:

- To understand that figures of speech appear to say one thing but mean another

- To use figures of speech correctly

Focus Activity:

Prepare pictures that illustrate figures of speech, such as "It's raining cats and dogs." Discuss what the words *say* and what they *mean*.

Process:

List figures of speech. Students recall those they have heard; teacher adds others.

Assignment:

Figures of Speech

Students select a figure of speech to use in a sentence, a paragraph, or a story. Write what it seems to mean and what it really means; illustrate. Examples:

- lower than a snake
- had cold feet
- down in the dumps
- barking up the wrong tree
- frog in his throat
- thorn in his side
- raining cats and dogs
- in the doghouse
- heart sank
- cried crocodile tears
- foot in his mouth

Simile Word Study

This is a good way to introduce or emphasize the *simile*. Examples:

- as sharp as a tack
- as sly as a fox
- as easy as apple pie
- as mad as an old wet hen
- as cool as a cucumber
- as red as fire
- like finding a needle in a haystack
- room looks like a junkyard

Extension:

Students add one or more words to complete the following statements.

- Mike's hair is as red as….
- A beetle looks like….
- The clouds look like….
- Anger is like….
- Fear is like….
- Bees sound like….
- A piece of chocolate candy is like….
- My little brother/sister is like….
- After running, my face is as red as….
- The ping pong ball jumps around like….
- My feet are as cold as….
- Happiness is like….
- School is like….
- Books are like….

Additional Short Assignments

1. Students remove shoes, trace one foot on construction paper, and cut out the design. On the design, write a story beginning: Someday I will be…. Place the stories on the bulletin board with the title "Steps to the Future."

   Other ideas for stories include "A Day in the Life of My (or a famous person's) Foot" and "Places My Foot Shouldn't Have Gone." This also works well with hand designs. Beginning lines: My hand reaches for….; One good thing about a hand is….; Helping hands….

2. Using an opaque projector, create a profile of each student. The story on the back should be titled, "All About Me." This makes a good gift for parents.

3. Write a story telling how your life would change if … telephones had two-way viewing capacity … the earth had no gravity … everyone had to travel by donkey or horseback … everyone suddenly started walking backwards.

4. Compare yourself or someone else to an insect. Illustrate.

5. Write a page in your pet's diary. Illustrate.

6. Apply the saying, "Curiosity killed the cat," to a time in your life.

7. Write a story titled "My first … (piano recital, dance, tee-ball game, ride on a roller coaster)." Illustrate.

8. Rewrite a favorite fairy tale as a poem.

9. List creatures with wings. Choose one and write a story about flying away.

10. Pretend you live inside your school desk or under your bed. Write a story about your experiences.

11. Pretend you are a flower. Write about the people who come by and how they treat you. Illustrate.

12. Design personal stationery and write a letter to someone.

13. Draw a map of an imaginary place. Write a story that takes place there.

14. Choose a picture from the picture file and write a story that tells what happened before and after the picture was taken.

15. Pretend you are an ant. Write a story about attending a picnic as an uninvited guest.

16. Imagine you are lost in a swamp. Tell about your adventures.

17. Imagine you are a balloon. Tell about the day you flew away. Where did you go? What did you see? How did the day end?

18. Write a classified ad to try to sell something you no longer need/want. Be descriptive but brief. Remember you must pay for each line.

19. Write a story based on a nursery rhyme (*Mary Had a Little Lamb, Little Bo Peep, Jack and Jill*).

20. List imaginative ways to travel (donkey, pogo stick, rocket). Choose one and write a story about traveling this way.

Collaborative Writing

Suggestions for Collaborative Classroom Writing

1. Develop a classroom (or grade) newspaper. Include news articles, a question/answer section (e.g., If you won a million dollars, what would you do?), birthday announcements, classified ads, interviews, jokes, a teacher of the week dedication, word puzzles, and more.

2. After studying root words, have students develop a classroom dictionary. They make their own words by combining root words, such as poly (many) + onym (name) = polyonyms (many names).

3. Allow students to collaborate (two or three students) on the Photo Essay assignments (see Creative Research Chapter, pp. 101-102).

4. Group project: Write a personality profile of a character from a story or book you read in class. One student can write each paragraph:

    • introduction
    • physical characteristics
    • emotional characteristics
    • how the character changed through the story

    Students then work together to complete the paper by working on transition sentences to join the paragraphs and writing the conclusion. Grading options: Give two grades (individual and group). Give all group members the same grade (automatic deduction of 10 points if students are off-task during work time).

5. Develop a classroom story. Plan the story together. Choose one student (perhaps the child with the longest name) to begin the story. Each student adds one or two sentences.

6. Using a familiar tune, such as "She'll Be Coming 'Round the Mountain," write lyrics for a song.

7. Have a contest to see which group can write the best class or school song. This can be sung to a familiar tune, or a student with music background might compose a tune. Select someone outside the school to judge the entries. Have small prizes for the winning group or arrange for the local paper to interview the group.

8. Have students collaborate to write a "This Is Your Life" segment for an adult in the school system. Students can interview the honoree and develop written discourse based on the questions/answers. Invite the honoree to attend a class session and have students present their writing (possibly with sound effects).

notes

notes

Creative Research

The Research Process

Objective:

- To develop a documented research paper

This unit is appropriate for introducing research to grades five and six. It includes four creative research topics. Make prior arrangements with the librarian for research time in the library. If possible, have research material available in the classroom; for example, have a book that gives the meaning of names for the research project assignment on pp. 102-103, item #4.

Focus Activity:

Display several types of research materials (magazines, newspapers, encyclopedias, resource books). Discuss types of information we get from various sources.

Process:

Show students a research paper and point out some of the citations. Discuss plagiarism and the importance of giving credit to the source. Discuss subjects students are interested in, and point out that material can be found on almost any topic. A minimum of three sources is sufficient for this assignment. Go through basic steps for research at the appropriate time: bibliography cards, note cards, works cited page, rough draft, final copy. Give students a photocopied time line listing check points for each step of the research process. For those students who will be conducting interviews, include correct interview techniques. Remind students that the interviewee is a reference and results of the interview should be placed on note cards.

Assignment:

Choose one of the following four assignments.

Photo Essays

A pictorial tour of your town

1. Research historical facts about your town.

2. Take pictures of some historical sites.

3. Conduct interviews with longtime citizens of your town. (Have available a list of prospective interviewees.)

4. Write a research paper. Be sure to identify all pictures and to give credit for any source you use, including your personal interview(s).

Career exploration

1. Research requirements for a career in which you are interested. Include a job description, education requirements, physical requirements, and salary prospects.

2. Take pictures of someone in this profession (at work if possible), and of the place of business.

3. Conduct an interview with this person.

4. Write a research paper. Be sure to identify all pictures and to give credit for any source you use, including your personal interview.

Offer suggestions for those easily accessible in your town: nurse, teacher, doctor, lawyer, clergyman or priest, rancher, bank personnel, secretary, sheriff, policeman, veterinarian, post office employee, farmer, school superintendent or administrator, businessman, etc. This can be the child's parent or other relative.

Personnel at your school

1. Choose one personnel position at your school in which you are interested (principal, counselor, teacher, librarian, secretary, custodian). Research requirements for this position. Include a job description, education requirements, physical requirements, and salary prospects.

2. Take pictures of the person you have chosen completing both job-related and recreational tasks.

3. Conduct an interview with this person.

4. Write research paper. Be sure to identify all pictures and to give credit for any source you use, including your personal interview.

Research Project

Research the day/year you were born

1. Collect personal data.

    • copy of your birth certificate
    • interview parents, grandparents, siblings, and friends
    • pictures

2. Collect data from other sources.

    • newspapers (local, regional, others)
    • magazines: information about what was happening in the world on the day you were born
    • encyclopedias and other informative material, such as an almanac

3. Gather information about what life was like at that time.

    • scientific
    • medical
    • new inventions
    • President of the United States
    • any other information you think is interesting
    • main events and unique details

4. Research the meaning of your name and ask your parents why they gave you that name.

5. Develop a family tree.

Research Evaluation

Research Paper Evaluation

Add totals together and divide by six to find student's score.

1. **Content** (100 points): Double this grade.   _____

    Criteria:

    - interest level
    - accurate facts
    - relevant information
    - well-developed introductory paragraph
    - varied types of sentences
    - relevant paragraphs
    - transitions
    - appropriate conclusion

2. **Documentation** (100 points)   _____

    Criteria:

    - correct parenthetical reference
    - correct number of sources (minimum of three)
    - all references listed on works cited page

3. **Works Cited Page** (100 points)   _____

    Criteria:

    - correct form
    - all parenthetical references listed on works cited page

4. **Mechanics** (100 points) _____

   Criteria:

   - sentence structure
   - spelling
   - appropriate style (bold, underline, italics)
   - punctuation
   - grammar

5. **Format** (100 points) _____

   Criteria:

   - title page (10 points)
   - outline with thesis statement (70 points)
   - pagination (10 points)
   - margins (5 points)
   - neatness (5 points)

notes

Student Handouts

Peer Response Groups

Student Handout 1
for Page 31

Evaluation Sheet

Date	Title of Paper	Strengths	Weaknesses

Peer Response Groups

Student Handout 2
for Page 31

Evaluation Sheet

Title _____

Author _____

Respondent _____

1. I enjoyed the paper because _____
   _____

2. The paper had a clear beginning, middle, and end.

   Strongly Agree   Agree   Disagree

   If you disagree, what should be strengthened and why?

   _____
   _____
   _____

3. The mechanics were: excellent   good   poor

4. Specific errors I detected were _____
   _____

5. The sentence structure was: strong   short, choppy   wordy

6. The author of this paper should correct the following specific errors (e.g., fragments, run-ons, verb forms):

   _____
   _____
   _____

©ECS Learning Systems, Inc., San Antonio, Texas   All rights reserved

Expository Writing

Student Handout 3
for Page 51

Planning Worksheet

A. Name of project _____

B. List the things you need.

   _____

   _____

C. List (in order) the steps you should follow. You may need more or less than 5.

   1. _____

   2. _____

   3. _____

   4. _____

   5. _____

D. List any problems you think you might have.

   1. _____

   2. _____

   3. _____

E. How will you correct the problems?

   1. _____

   2. _____

   3. _____

Writing Books

Student Handout 4
for Page 63

Planning Sheet

Title _____

Author(s) _____

Type of Book _____

Setting:
      Time _____

      Place _____

Characters:
      Protagonist _____

      Antagonist _____

      Others _____

Conflict (problem) _____

_____

Plot Development (use short phrases):

      Exposition _____

      Rising Action _____

_____

      Climax _____

_____

      Falling Action _____

_____

      Resolution _____

Poetry

Student Handout 5
for Pages 21 & 72

Poetry Forms

Formula poems follow a set pattern.

Haiku: The haiku is a Japanese poem in three lines of 5, 7, and 5 syllables; it can be about a variety of subjects. It creates a picture and makes the reader feel emotion, such as joy or sadness.

Cinquain: The cinquain consists of five lines.

Line 1: one word (noun) to give the title
Line 2: two words to describe the title
Line 3: three words to express action concerning the title
Line 4: four words to express feeling(s) about the title
Line 5: one word that is a synonym for the title

Diamente: The diamente is a seven-line contrast poem that is set up to appear in a diamond shape on paper.

Line 1: one word (a noun, the subject)
Line 2: two words (adjectives describing line 1)
Line 3: three words ("ing" or "ed" words that relate to line 1)
Line 4: four words (first two nouns relate to line 1; second two nouns relate to line 7)
Line 5: three words ("ing" or "ed" words that relate to line 7)
Line 6: two words (adjectives describing line 7)
Line 7: one word (noun that is the opposite of line 1)

Contrast in thought occurs in line 4. Most people find it easier to start with lines 1 and 7.

Metaphor/Simile: A *metaphor* is a comparison between two things which does not use "like" or "as" but rather takes the form of a direct statement. Example: Anger is a raging fire. A *simile* is a comparison between two things; they are linked with "like" or "as." Example: Sadness is like a heavy cloud.

Metaphor/Simile Poem: The *metaphor* poem and the *simile* poem follow the same pattern. Note the difference in the last line.

Line 1: noun (also the title)
Lines 2-4: something about the subject (Each line should describe the subject in a different way.)
Line 5: a *metaphor* that begins with the noun from line 1
Line 5: a *simile* that begins with the noun from line 1 and includes "like" or "as"

Limerick: A limerick is a five-line nonsense poem, written in anapestic lines. An anapest is a metrical foot of three syllables, with two unaccented syllables followed by an accented one. The first, second, and fifth lines rhyme and consist of three feet. The third and fourth lines rhyme and consist of two feet. You can allow your imagination to run wild and even create your own words!

Shaped Whimsy: The Shaped Whimsy is an imaginative form of poetry. In this form, the poem is printed within a certain shape or in a certain design which reflects the subject of the poem. For example, the shape of a cloud might contain a poem about a cloudy day. Keep the shape simple.

Part-of-Speech Poem

Line 1: article (a, an, the) + noun
Line 2: adjective + conjunction + adjective
Line 3: verb + conjunction + verb
Line 4: adverb
Line 5: noun relating to the noun in the first line

Five-Senses Poem: This poem, which deals with an emotion, is developed by using the five senses. Choose an emotion such as happiness, sadness, love, hate, etc.

Line 1: color of the emotion
Line 2: sound of the emotion
Line 3: taste of the emotion
Line 4: smell of the emotion
Line 5: sight (what the emotion looks like)
Line 6: feeling evoked by the emotion

"I Am" Poem

Line 1: My name is....
Line 2: I am.... (3 words that describe you)
Line 3: I like.... (2 things such as food or sports)
Line 4: I can.... (2 things you feel you do well such as playing the piano, playing ball, etc.)
Lines 5-7: I wish I could (a) go.... (b) change.... (c) learn....
Line 8: Someday I will be....

Poem About Someone Else

Title
Line 1: (Name of person) is.... (color)
Line 2: (S/he) feels like.... (touch)
Line 3: (S/he) smells like....
Line 4: (S/he) reminds me of.... (story, song)
Line 5: (Name of person) is.... (noun: friend, relative, etc.)

Name Poem: Name poems are written using acrostic format. Use the letters of a name for the first letter of each line. Each line then tells something about the person.

Other Poetic Devices

Alliteration: repeating the initial letter or sound within the line. Key to remember: the word a*ll*iteration repeats the same letter. Examples: softly shining sea; cute cuddly kittens

Onomatopoeia: using words with sounds that tell their meaning. Examples: snakes *hiss*; bees *buzz*, cymbals *clang*; birds *chirp*

Couplet: two lines of verse with rhyming end word

Free Verse: Verse that is free of the restrainsts of meter. There are three basic types of free verse poetry.

1. End-stopped verse makes a line break at the point of a natural pause. Example: Walt Whitman's "Song of Myself."

2. Run-on verse usually makes a line break where there is no grammatical or syntactical pause, such as breaking between adjectives and nouns. This type of verse encourages shorter lines that depend on the next line for completion of a thought. Example: Maya Angelou's "Forgive."

3. Visual or spatial verse creates a visible picture as well as a word picture. (Refer to example for Shaped Whimsy.) Example:
>   Night drops gently
>   over
>   one side of the earth,
>   leaving the other
>   luminous.

Poetry Notebook

Student Handout 6
for Page 73

Assignment: Create a colorful, illustrated poetry notebook. It must contain the following sections.

Cover (design as you wish)

1. Original name for your notebook
2. Your name and grade level
3. The date

Specified Poems (Part I): Write an original poem for each of the following types of poetry.

- Haiku
- Cinquain
- Metaphor Poem
- Simile Poem
- Limerick
- Shaped Whimsy
- Name Poem
- Part-of-Speech Poem
- Five-senses Poem
- "I Am" Poem
- Poem About Someone Else
- Rhyming couplets

Specified Poems (Part II): Follow instructions for the following poems. These can be rhyming, free verse, or formula poems.

- Alliteration: 2-line poem using alliteration in first line
- Onomatopoeia: poem using at least 1 or 2 examples of onomatopoeia
- Poem about your favorite person or pet (4 or more lines)
- Poem about your "security blanket" or favorite toy when you were younger
- 4-line poem beginning with one of the following lines:

    Someday I'll be….
    I wish I could go….
    My imaginary friend and I….
    The greatest gift I could give….
    I lost my….
    When I was a baby….

Add as many original poems as you wish. You may write other poems based on the instructions in Section I, as well as free verse poems, or rhyming poems.

notes

Student Work

Writing Stages

Student Work 1 for Page 16

Writing Samples:
(original spelling and punctuation)

Chloe Watson, K, school year 1996-97 (note from teacher, fill in the blanks)

My name is *CHlOe*.

because (filled in by parents) *the unique name seemed to fit her. She looked like a Chloe, not a Micah, Reagan, or any of the several other names we had selected prior to her birth. When we held her after she was born, and said the other names, they did not fit, but Chloe did.*

In her journal, Chloe dictated some things to her teacher. Example: I like the clouds. I like the blue sky. I like my bed. In addition, she drew several pictures and began to write some words.

Seth Watson, grade 1, 1996-97 school year (journal entries)

9/9/96: I was at a fotball game and a man got hrt hey had to lay on a cot.

9/96: (copied) Just as Moses LiFted up the Snake in the desert so the SUN of Man Must be lifted up that everyone who believs in him

8/96: today i plad socor it wos fun today i got to play the game and today I dug a hol with Jordan i got to fit with INdiN

1/9/97: My Name is Seth Alan. Win I grow up ol bey a football playor i will play for texis tech in collig then i will play for the Lions forst then Cowboys and then Dolphins I will play my best.

Hanna Watson, grade 1, 1994-95 school year (journal entries)

9/27/94: (In response to prompt, "If I Had a Pet") Story plus illustration: I had a pet. But I had to giv it a way. It is a grul. Her name is Mady. I love Mady. She is a gud dog. I mis hur Wawa!! I git to see her. I miyet get to get a noo pet. I thec that I will git a rabbit.

12/9/94: Christmas - Meny meny yiurs a go wen Jesus wus born. that is haw we got Christmas. Santa has 9 reindeer. Haing your stocing.

1/3/95: My New Year's Resolutions are to study more. To love more. To red more. To mide more. To stop eteing so much shooger. Pic-up more. I will fold cloes. I'm going to write more.

2/27/95 (describing favorite part of a book): I likr it bee cos on that page Grampy gis in the water and pools them bac to shor.

Grade 2
1995-96 school year (journal entries)

8/23/95: My Moms name is Kim. She is PTA Presudint. She is a good Mom. One uv my sisters is Chloe she likes to play haws. She likes art. I have a nuter siter her name is Emma. We have sumthing we call a wa-wa it is a pasy (Emma's pacifier). My Dad's name is Ed.

4/17/96: My dog is an old dog. he's fat, tall and flufey. His name in Muffey. He lays arond all day long. And does evreything wrong. But, I still love him. He rolls in the dert. And messis up moms new scurt. He chuwes up my homwork. He messis up my bick. But, I still love him. He chuwes up my Dads work papers. He leves fur all arond the house. He dos not run after a mouse. But, I still Love him. Why you ask? cause He is min.

Grade 3
1996-97 school year

10/15/96:   Roses are red,
Volets are blue,
this poem has a new
home with you!

Poetry

Student Work 2
Page 72

Haiku

Emma excitedly
Watches for the white pickup
Runs to meet Daddy

Beautiful flowers
Shimmering in the sunlight
Colorful and bright

Cinquain

Alexandra
Tiny, beautiful
Smiles, eats, sleeps
Makes our family happy
Baby

Diamente

Summer
Short, hot
Swimming, playing, reading
Vacation, baseball, hockey, school
Studying, freezing, skiing
Long, cold
Winter

Metaphor/Simile

Joy
Makes me feel happy
Keeps me warm inside
Brings smiles to others
Joy is a day of sunshine. (metaphor)
Joy is like a day of sunshine. (simile)

Limerick

There was once a big rhino named Sue
Who just did not know what she must do.
So when others would play,
She would just run away,
And so now Sue must live in a zoo.

Shaped Whimsy

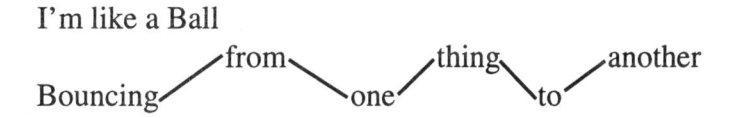

I'm like a Ball
Bouncing ╱from╲ ╱thing╲ ╱another
         ╲one╱   ╲to╱

Part-of-Speech Poem

A child
Adorable and beautiful
Growing and learning
Always
Samantha

Five-Senses Poem

Happiness is pink.
It sounds like nuts.
It tastes like candy.
It smells like egg.
It looks like a circle.
Happiness makes me smile. (Jordan Watson, K, dictated)

Anger is as red as a fire engine.
It sounds like chopping a tree down
And tastes as hot as a chili pepper.
It smells like stinky feet
And looks like someone shooting an animal that's becoming extinct.
Anger makes me feel like I want to kick and punch someone. (Hanna Watson, grade 3)

"I Am" Poem

My name is Seth.
I am tough, fast, and smart.
I like football and spaghetti.
I can wrestle and shoot the ball.
I wish I could
go to Disney World;
change problems for sad people;
learn Karate.
Someday I will be a professional football player. (Seth Watson, grade 1, dictated)

Poem About Someone Else

Martha
Martha is soft pink
Like a fluffy blanket.
She is cuddly as a baby rabbit.
And smells like baby powder.
She reminds me of "Lullaby."
Martha is my baby sister.

Name Poem

Cute
Happy
Loving
Observant
Energetic

Joyful
Occasionally daydreams
Respectful
Darling
Agreeable
Nearly six

Alliteration

Madison makes magic moments
Playing "Pretend" with her sister
Singing sweetly to her babies
Praying her good night prayers.

Onomatopoeia

The bees buzzed loudly
As the bear searched for honey.
Ouch! Too late now!

Couplets

Humpty Dumpty sat on a wall,
Humpty Dumpty had a great fall.
All the king's horses and all the king's men
Couldn't put Humpty together again.

Free Verse

Hanna Watson (grade 3) wrote the following poem on the computer and printed it in colors, illustrating the thoughts (original spelling).

THE EVERGLADES

I am the Everglades, (dark green)
I have a lot of animals such
as the Blue Haron, (blue)
funny plants like the
Mangrow tree, (light green)
and a lot of marshy dirty
waters that my allagaters swim in. (brown)

notes

About the Authors

Patricia (Pat) Watson earned a Bachelor of Music Education degree from Eastern New Mexico University and acquired graduate hours and further certification at Texas Tech University. During 21 years of teaching, Pat worked at the elementary, junior high, and high school levels. For 10 years, she taught English III, creative writing, and literary genres at Muleshoe High School in Muleshoe, Texas. She was named Muleshoe ISD Teacher of the Year in May, 1993, and Region XVII Secondary Teacher of the Year in August, 1993. Although she retired from classroom teaching in 1994, Pat continues to present workshops and publish instructional material for teachers. Pat has been married to W.T. Watson for 43 years. They have three sons, David, Ed, and Cliff, and 11 grandchildren.

Janet (Nix) Watson graduated from Texas Tech University in 1986 with a Bachelor of Science in Elementary Education. She taught third grade for 3 years in the Longview ISD. During that time, she saw a steady increase in the TAAS scores for her students and attributes much of their improvement to consistent journal writing. Janet and her husband, Cliff, live in Tyler, Texas, where two of their children attend school. A full-time homemaker and mother to Seth, Jordan Elise, Madison, and Alexandra, Janet plans to return to the classroom some day.